YIELDED ONE

PONDERINGS ON PATIENCE
SARAH CAROLINE RANSOM

"THE HEAVENLY FATHER DOES NOT ASK FOR GOLDEN VESSELS. HE DOES NOT ASK FOR SILVER VESSELS. GOD ASKS FOR YIELDED VESSELS."

KATHRYN KUHLMAN.

WHAT FOLLOWS ARE PONDERINGS & PRAYERS, THAT HAVE COME FROM THE TENSION OF WAITING, REFINEMENT, URGENCY, ALL THINGS SLOW, THE MYSTERY OF TIME AND MARVELS OF THE INCREDIBLY CLOSE GOD. THE LORD SHEPHERDS OUR HEARTS IN A WAY THAT SOMETIMES CONTRADICTS OUR PRESENT SURROUNDINGS.. I AM IN AWE OF THE FACT THAT IN A SHAKING WORLD, WHERE CHANGE IS CRAVED, AND THE FRUIT OF HEAVEN IS DESIRED, THE FATHER IS NOT DEMANDING US TO PRODUCE IT.. BUT TO BELIEVE AND REMAIN IN HIS TRUTH.

HOWEVER,

HE KNOWS THE OVERFLOW OF A YIELDED AND CAPTIVATED HEART WILL LEAVE NOTHING UNTOUCHED IN ITS WAKE. WOULD OUR YIELDING TO HIM ACCELERATE HEAVEN ON EARTH.

TABLE OF CONTENTS

ONE: TRANSITION
TWO: FORWARD
THREE: WINTER
FOUR: POURED
FIVE: LIGHT
SIX: ASK
SEVEN: UNWRITTEN
EIGHT: ANTICIPATION
NINE: EXCELLENT
TEN: BREAD

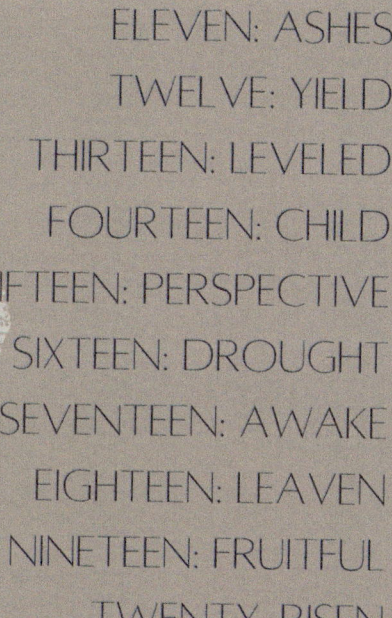

ELEVEN: ASHES
TWELVE: YIELD
THIRTEEN: LEVELED
FOURTEEN: CHILD
FIFTEEN: PERSPECTIVE
SIXTEEN: DROUGHT
SEVENTEEN: AWAKE
EIGHTEEN: LEAVEN
NINETEEN: FRUITFUL
TWENTY: RISEN

ONE

TRANSITION

PRODUCTIVE PAIN
THE WAY OF REDEMPTION
THROUGH
NOT AROUND
FELT
NOT IGNORED
A PILGRIMAGE
OF DAILY DEATH
I SURRENDER
WHAT I THINK
ARRIVAL IS

"HE BELIEVED, HOPING AGAINST HOPE, SO THAT HE BECAME THE FATHER OF MANY NATIONS, ACCORDING TO WHAT HAD BEEN SPOKEN: SO WILL YOUR DESCENDANTS BE. HE DID NOT WEAKEN IN FAITH WHEN HE CONSIDERED HIS OWN BODY TO BE ALREADY DEAD (SINCE HE WAS ABOUT A HUNDRED YEARS OLD) AND ALSO THE DEADNESS OF SARAH'S WOMB. HE DID NOT WAVER IN UNBELIEF AT GOD'S PROMISE BUT WAS STRENGTHENED IN HIS FAITH AND GAVE GLORY TO GOD, BECAUSE HE WAS FULLY CONVINCED THAT WHAT GOD HAD PROMISED, HE WAS ALSO ABLE TO DO."

ROMANS 4:18–21

FORWARD

EYES ON YOU
WAVE WALKING
BRACING FOR IMPACT
LIGHTNING AND THUNDER
TRIED THEIR BEST TO TAUNT AND TEASE
HOWEVER, MY HEART STEADIED
YOU ARE WITH ME
NOT LOOKING TO THE
LEFT OR RIGHT
GOING AFRAID
THE IN FRONT OF ME PROTECTOR
& SIDE BY SIDE FRIEND
MOVING FORWARD
FROM THE MIDNIGHT

"LORD, IF IT'S YOU," PETER ANSWERED HIM, "COMMAND ME TO COME TO YOU ON THE WATER."

HE SAID, "COME."

AND CLIMBING OUT OF THE BOAT, PETER STARTED WALKING ON THE WATER AND CAME TOWARD JESUS. BUT WHEN HE SAW THE STRENGTH OF THE WIND, HE WAS AFRAID, AND BEGINNING TO SINK HE CRIED OUT, "LORD, SAVE ME!"

IMMEDIATELY JESUS REACHED OUT HIS HAND, CAUGHT HOLD OF HIM, AND SAID TO HIM, "YOU OF LITTLE FAITH, WHY DID YOU DOUBT?"

WHEN THEY GOT INTO THE BOAT, THE WIND CEASED. THEN THOSE IN THE BOAT WORSHIPED HIM AND SAID, "TRULY YOU ARE THE SON OF GOD."

MATTHEW 14:22-33

FROM THE REVELATION OF WHO YOU ARE, LORD,
LET US BE WAVE WALKERS, FOREVER AND EVER

THREE

WINTER

OH THE REVELATION
HIDDEN IN THE WINTER
WHAT CAN BE SEEN
THROUGH THE BARREN
THE COMING SPRING
A PROMISED NEWNESS
IF IT WEREN'T SO BARREN
SO CLEAR
I WOULD HAVE MISSED IT

HOLY SPIRIT, COMFORTER, IN WHATEVER WINTER
MAY BE PRESENT, BARRENNESS, BITTERNESS,
LONGING, HIDDENNESS....

COME

FOUR

POURED

WOUNDED ONE
LIFE POURED OUT TO GROUND
THE HARVEST COMES
FROM SHED BLOOD
THE WISEST MEN
CONFOUND

"BUT NOW IN CHRIST JESUS, YOU WHO WERE FAR AWAY HAVE BEEN BROUGHT NEAR BY THE BLOOD OF CHRIST. FOR HE IS OUR PEACE, WHO MADE BOTH GROUPS ONE AND TORE DOWN THE DIVIDING WALL OF HOSTILITY. IN HIS FLESH, HE MADE OF NO EFFECT THE LAW CONSISTING OF COMMANDS AND EXPRESSED IN REGULATIONS, SO THAT HE MIGHT CREATE IN HIMSELF ONE NEW MAN FROM THE TWO, RESULTING IN PEACE. HE DID THIS SO THAT HE MIGHT RECONCILE BOTH TO GOD IN ONE BODY THROUGH THE CROSS BY WHICH HE PUT THE HOSTILITY TO DEATH. HE CAME AND PROCLAIMED THE GOOD NEWS OF PEACE TO YOU WHO WERE FAR AWAY AND PEACE TO THOSE WHO WERE NEAR. FOR THROUGH HIM WE BOTH HAVE ACCESS IN ONE SPIRIT TO THE FATHER."

EPHESIANS 2:13–18

YOUR NEARNESS , OUR HARVEST

FIVE

LIGHT

LIGHT AND FLEETING
ACTUALLY ERASED
YOU SAY
IS THE STING OF DEATH
ALTHOUGH IT MAY LINGER
FOR A WHILE LONGER
UNFATHOMABLE GOODNESS
THAT COMES FROM THE
WOUNDING
WILL SOON BE UNEARTHED
AND BROUGHT TO LIGHT

"THEREFORE WE DO NOT GIVE UP. EVEN THOUGH OUR OUTER PERSON IS BEING DESTROYED, OUR INNER PERSON IS BEING RENEWED DAY BY DAY. FOR OUR MOMENTARY LIGHT AFFLICTION IS PRODUCING FOR US AN ABSOLUTELY INCOMPARABLE ETERNAL WEIGHT OF GLORY. SO WE DO NOT FOCUS ON WHAT IS SEEN, BUT ON WHAT IS UNSEEN. FOR WHAT IS SEEN IS TEMPORARY, BUT WHAT IS UNSEEN IS ETERNAL."

2 CORINTHIANS 4:16–18

ASK

YOU HAVE THE AUDACITY TO ASK
WHAT DO I WANT DONE
WHAT DO I LONG TO SEE ACCOMPLISHED
WHAT DO I DESIRE
WHAT DO I ACHE FOR
WHAT DO I NEED TO BE HEALED
WHY DO YOU ASK
WHAT YOU ALREADY KNOW THE ANSWER TO
MORE JEALOUS FOR MY WHOLENESS
THAN I COULD EVER BE
SON OF MAN
YOU HAVE NO RESERVATIONS
SON OF GOD
YOU HAVE NO LIMITATIONS
MY SILENCE
MY DISTANCE
ARE WHAT
PROLONG THE OPEN HEAVEN
ALL YOU WANTED WAS ME TO ASK

"WHAT DO YOU WANT ME TO DO FOR YOU?" JESUS ASKED HIM. THE BLIND MAN SAID, "RABBI, I WANT TO SEE." "GO," SAID JESUS, "YOUR FAITH HAS HEALED YOU." IMMEDIATELY HE RECEIVED HIS SIGHT AND FOLLOWED JESUS ALONG THE ROAD.
MARK 10:51–52

HEART,
I URGE YOU TO ASK
I DARE YOU TO WAIT

SEVEN

UNWRITTEN

I MAY NEVER SEE THE EVIDENCE
OF MY SURRENDER
AND YET
WITH CONFIDENCE IN MY ETERNAL GOD
COMES A WAVERING OF WHAT I WANT
ON THE LEFT SIDE OF A SEMICOLON
I WAIT
KNOWING THAT YOU WILL WRITE THE RIGHT SIDE
DEATH SAID THE SENTENCE IS OVER
YET THE SENTENCE OF YOUR DEATH
AND VICTORY OVER IT
TURNS A NEW PAGE
FOR THE UNFINISHED STORY
TO BE WRITTEN

I RECENTLY HAD THE REVELATION THAT CERTAINTY IS OVERRATED... IT REQUIRES NO FAITH. I WANT TO PLEASE GOD. FAITH PLEASES GOD. I SEE IN THE WORD OF GOD THAT THOSE WHO THROW CERTAINTY OUT AND RUN TOWARDS THE UNKNOWN IN FAITH ALWAYS END UP HELD IN THE SAFETY OF HIS MYSTERY.

TREAD GLADLY ON THE NARROW ROAD WITH
CONFIDENT IGNORANCE

ANTICIPATION

YOU ARE GOOD
IF NOTHING CHANGES
IF NOTHING STAYS THE SAME
I HOLD MY BREATH
YOU FILL MY LUNGS
WITH A FRESH WIND
TO WAIT AND BE MADE READY

HOW TO LIVE IN THE TENSION OF THE IN-BETWEEN... THE CRYING OUT TO GOD... MIMICKING GETHSEMANE PRAYERS OF WHOLE HEARTED SURRENDER AND BOLD ASKING JESUS SHOWED US. HE ASKED THE CREATOR OF THE UNIVERSE IF HE DIDN'T HAVE TO DO THE ONE THING HE CAME TO DO.. I'VE WRESTLED WITH SHAME ASKING FOR RIDICULOUS THINGS AND THE REGRET OF NOT APPROACHING HIM WITH THE UNVEILED FACE I HAVE BEFORE HIM. HOW DO I CARRY THE TENSION OF ANTICIPATION AND SURRENDER? MAYBE WE AREN'T SUPPOSE TO. IT LEAVES US UTTERLY DESPERATE FOR COMMUNION WITH HIM,

---

WHICH ULTIMATELY ISN'T THAT WHAT WE'RE MADE FOR?

NINE

EXCELLENT

JUST ONE MUSTARD SEED
TO A FORREST OF TREES
YOU DO ALL THINGS WELL
AND IT'S RIDICULOUS

AGAIN, LEAVING THE REGION OF TYRE, HE WENT BY WAY OF SIDON TO THE SEA OF GALILEE, THROUGH THE REGION OF THE DECAPOLIS. THEY BROUGHT TO HIM A DEAF MAN WHO HAD DIFFICULTY SPEAKING AND BEGGED JESUS TO LAY HIS HAND ON HIM. SO HE TOOK HIM AWAY FROM THE CROWD IN PRIVATE. AFTER PUTTING HIS FINGERS IN THE MAN'S EARS AND SPITTING, HE TOUCHED HIS TONGUE. LOOKING UP TO HEAVEN, HE SIGHED DEEPLY AND SAID TO HIM, "EPHPHATHA!" (THAT IS, "BE OPENED!"). IMMEDIATELY HIS EARS WERE OPENED, HIS TONGUE WAS LOOSENED, AND HE BEGAN TO SPEAK CLEARLY. HE ORDERED THEM TO TELL NO ONE, BUT THE MORE HE ORDERED THEM, THE MORE THEY PROCLAIMED IT.

THEY WERE EXTREMELY ASTONISHED AND SAID, "HE HAS DONE EVERYTHING WELL. HE EVEN MAKES THE DEAF HEAR AND THE MUTE SPEAK."
       MARK 7:31-37

EVEN JUST A SIGH UNTO THE ONE WHO DOES EVERYTHING WELL, IS HEARD AND MOVED UPON BY THE GREAT CREATOR GOD

ABSURD

TEN

BREAD

JESUS, "THE I AM WITH YOU ALWAYS" FEAST
NOT JUST THE ENOUGH BUT THE ONE WHO OVER-DELIVERERS
THE ABUNDANT ONE
NOT JUST WHAT IS NEEDED
BUT WHAT WE DESIRE
YOU ARE THE FRESH FULFILLING BREAD,
MADE AVAILABLE
BREATH BY BREATH
MOMENT BY MOMENT
NEW MERCIES TO APPROACH THE TABLE
YOU ARE WAITING
LONGING FOR US TO COME
COME HUNGRY FOR MORE
THE MORE WE DIDN'T EVEN KNOW WAS POSSIBLE
SORROW AND SIGHING FLEE
HOPELESSNESS AND DESPAIR DEPART
AS WE SIT AND DINE
AND REST IN YOUR FINISHED WORK
IN THE WAITING, THERE IS ABUNDANCE
JESUS OUR ETERNAL LIFE,
NOT JUST IN THE ONE TO COME
BUT NOW
RIGHT NOW, THIS VERY BREATH
IS THE DAY OF HIS BODY BROKEN
FOR THE JOY SET BEFORE HIM
WE TASTE AND SEE OF HIS GOODNESS
YOU FILL US UP AND NOW THE JOY SET BEFORE US
IS TO KEEP HUNGERING
KEEP LONGING
UNTIL OUR FAITH IS MADE SIGHT
FOR THE KING AND
KINGDOM COME
BREAD OF LIFE
WE HUNGER FOR YOU

"A ROAD WILL BE THERE AND A WAY;
IT WILL BE CALLED THE HOLY WAY.
THE UNCLEAN WILL NOT TRAVEL ON IT,
BUT IT WILL BE FOR THE ONE WHO WALKS THE PATH.
FOOLS WILL NOT WANDER ON IT.
THERE WILL BE NO LION THERE,
AND NO VICIOUS BEAST WILL GO UP ON IT;
THEY WILL NOT BE FOUND THERE.
BUT THE REDEEMED WILL WALK ON IT,
AND THE RANSOMED OF THE LORD WILL RETURN
AND COME TO ZION WITH SINGING,
CROWNED WITH UNENDING JOY.
JOY AND GLADNESS WILL OVERTAKE THEM,
AND SORROW AND SIGHING WILL FLEE.

ISAIAH 35:8–10

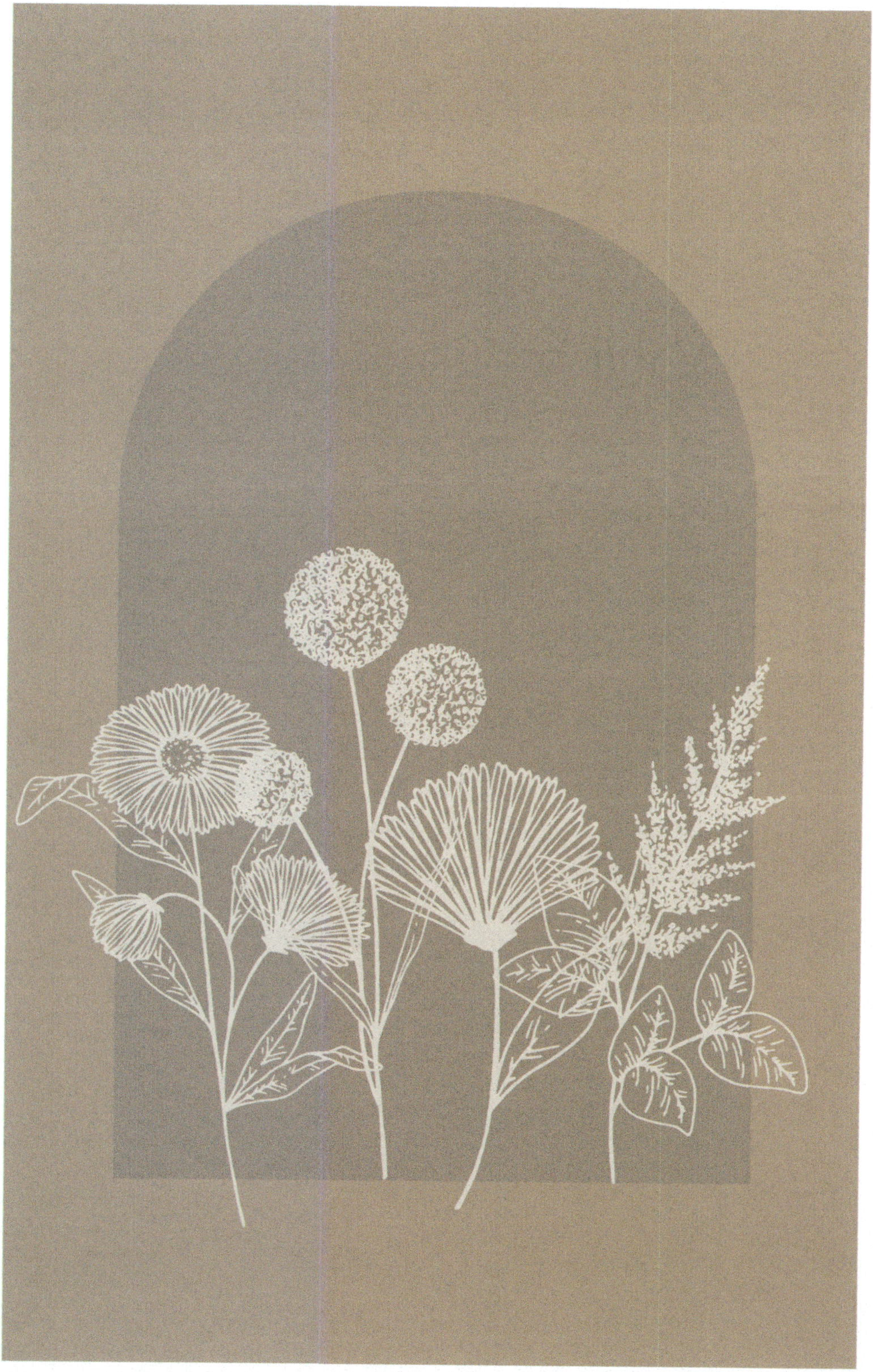

ELEVEN

ASHES

YOU MAKE DESOLATION FRUITFUL
HOW CAN IT BE
YOUR TIMELESS LOVE
REACHES FAR BEYOND THE TOMB I SIT AT
YET YOU RESOLVE TO SHOULDER MY
WEARY WEEPINGS
YOUR RESURRECTION POWER
YIELDED TO THE FULFILLMENT OF MY FEELINGS
YOUR AWARENESS OF MY PAIN, MATCHLESS
YOUR CONFIDENCE OF THE LIFE TO COME IS OFFENSIVE
ABSENT OF IMPATIENCE
NOT HURRIED TO PERFORM THE MIRACLE YOU ARE ABLE
OVERWHELMED BY THE PERMISSION YOU GIVE
TO SIT WITH THE ASHES AND FEEL
FOR MOMENTS LONGER

LOSS AND LONGING HAVE TAUGHT ME THAT GOD IS MORE THAN JUST A TEACHER. I HAVE HAD TO RENEW MY MIND TO THE TRUTH THAT HIS LOVING NATURE NEVER CHANGES... THE SUFFERING WE WALK THROUGH ISN'T SOME TWISTED WAY TO "LEARN A LESSON" .. HE IS REVELATION HIMSELF.. HE IS LIVING AND MOVING, RESTORING, DRAWING NEAR RIGHT NOW.. WITHOUT ANY ASSISTANCE FROM US.

.

WHERE DID I PICK UP THE LIE THAT ALL HE WANTS TO DO IS CORRECT AND TEACH THROUGH THE PAIN OF THIS BROKEN WORLD. HE DIDN'T CREATE A BROKEN WORLD. YET MADE A WAY FOR BROKEN THINGS TO BE MADE WHOLE

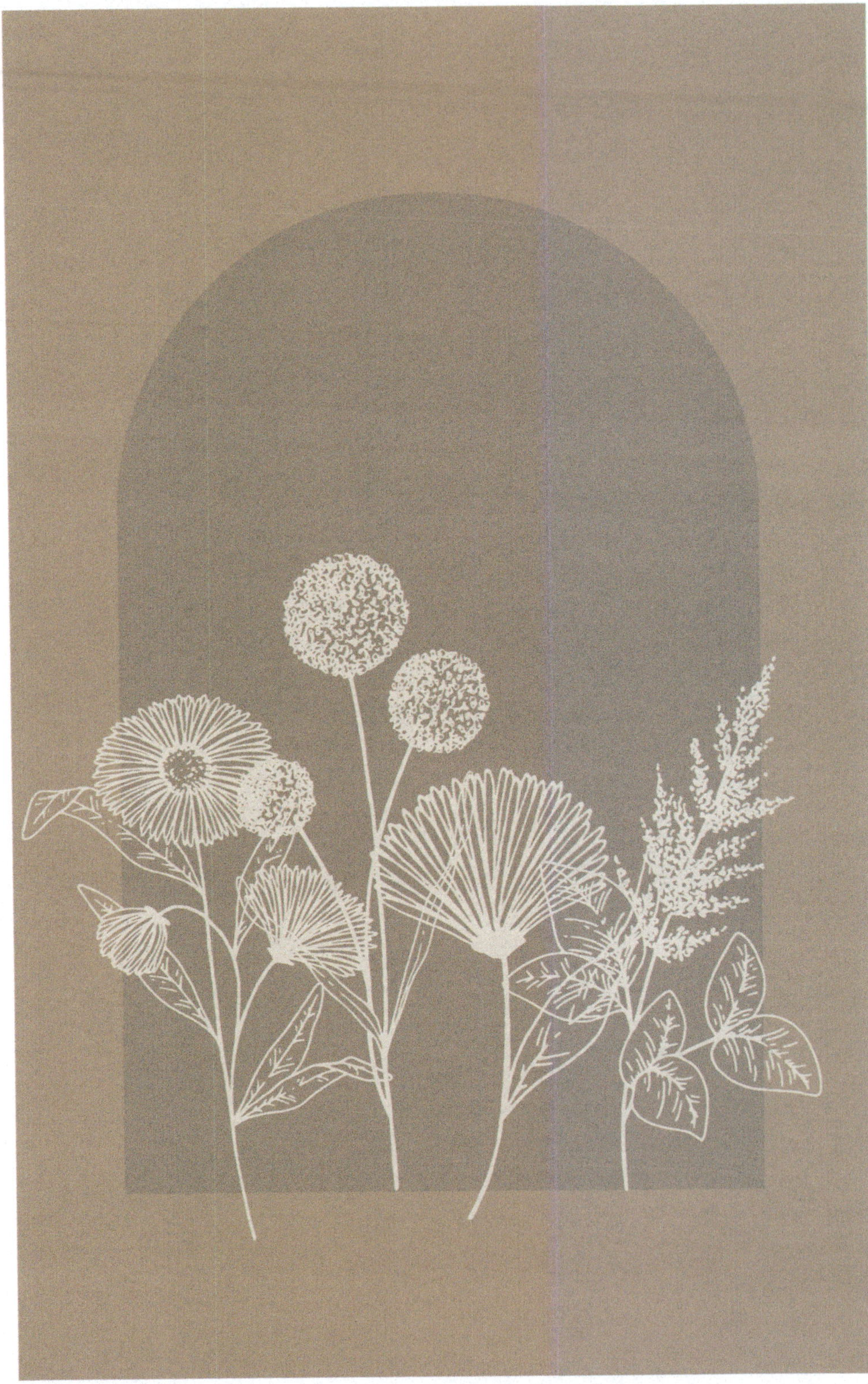

TWELVE

YIELD

AND IF THIS IS SO,
HEART,
WAIT
IN EXPECTANT & MEEK
SILENCE
WITH A YIELDED WILL,
TO THE GOODNESS
OF HIS WAYS

IN THE BEGINNING, HE OFFERED FULLNESS OF LIFE..

IN THE MIDDLE HE IS RESURRECTION LIFE

IN THE END HE IS ETERNAL LIFE

LIFE IS A PERSON, WHO WANTS TO SIT BESIDE YOU

AND A HEART YIELDED TO HIM
WILL DO GREATER THINGS

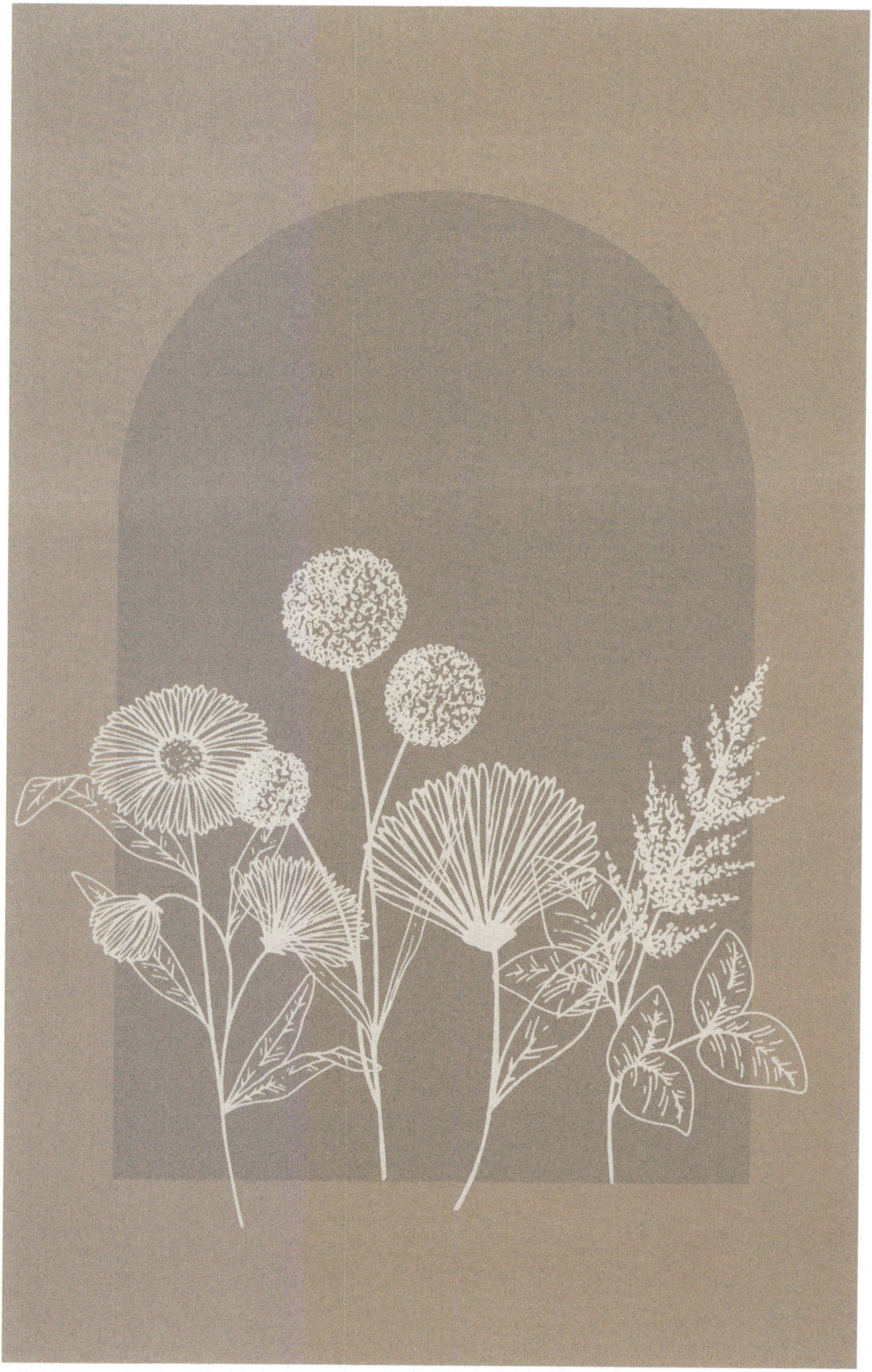

THIRTEEN

LEVELED

THE DISMAY OF A
COURSE CORRECTION
THE LEVELING OF
A BUILT UP DREAM
WE LAID EACH BRICK TOGETHER
I AM CERTAIN
NOTHING IN VAIN OR WASTED
JUST MORE TIME WITH YOU
NOW WE STEP OVER
THE RUBLE OF WHAT WAS
AND PREPARE A HIGHWAY
WITH THE BROKEN THINGS
AND WAIT
FOR YOUR PROMISED RESTORATION

A PERSON'S STEPS ARE ESTABLISHED BY THE LORD,
AND HE TAKES PLEASURE IN HIS WAY.
THOUGH HE FALLS, HE WILL NOT BE OVERWHELMED,
BECAUSE THE LORD SUPPORTS HIM WITH HIS HAND.

I HAVE BEEN YOUNG AND NOW I AM OLD,
YET I HAVE NOT SEEN THE RIGHTEOUS ABANDONED
OR HIS CHILDREN BEGGING FOR BREAD.

HE IS ALWAYS GENEROUS, ALWAYS LENDING,
AND HIS CHILDREN ARE A BLESSING.

PSALM 37:23–26

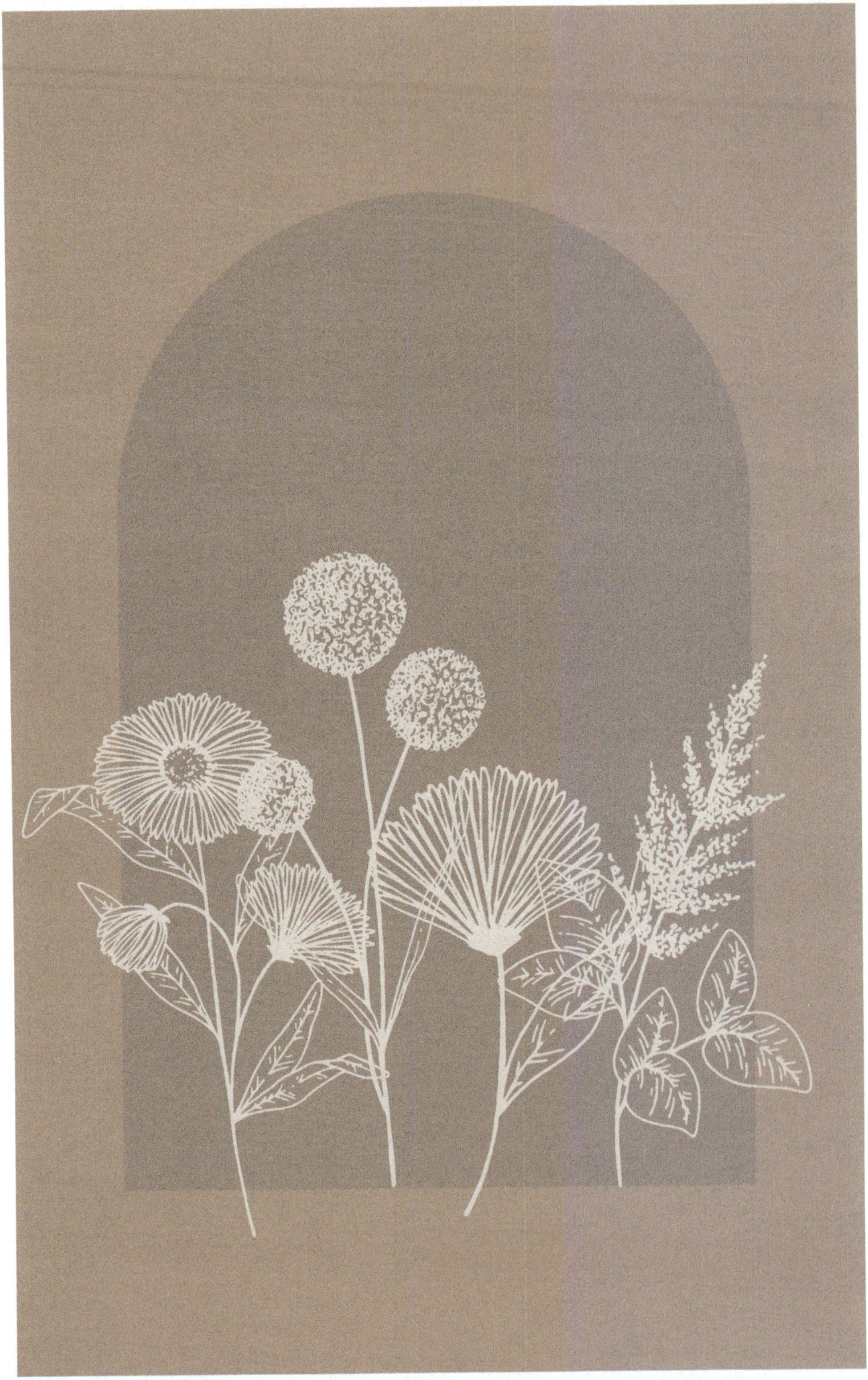

FOURTEEN

CHILD

LIKE A CHILD
BURIED INTO A FATHER'S CHEST
MY ARRESTED EMOTIONS
REST AND WAIT
IN THE SAFETY OF YOUR ARMS
I ASK FOR MORE
KNOWING YOU HEAR MY WHISPERED REQUESTS
BEFORE I'VE EVEN SPOKEN A
SYLLABLE OF DESPERATION

"LORD, MY HEART IS NOT PROUD;
MY EYES ARE NOT HAUGHTY.
I DO NOT GET INVOLVED WITH THINGS
TOO GREAT OR TOO WONDROUS FOR ME.

INSTEAD, I HAVE CALMED AND QUIETED MY SOUL
LIKE A WEANED CHILD WITH ITS MOTHER;
MY SOUL IS LIKE A WEANED CHILD.

ISRAEL, PUT YOUR HOPE IN THE LORD,
BOTH NOW AND FOREVER."
PSALMS 131:1-3

FATHER, GIVE OUR HEARTS THE REVELATION OF A HOPE THAT CHANGES EVERYTHING. WOULD WE BE TETHERED TO THE LIVING HOPE & RIPPED FROM THE FLEETING

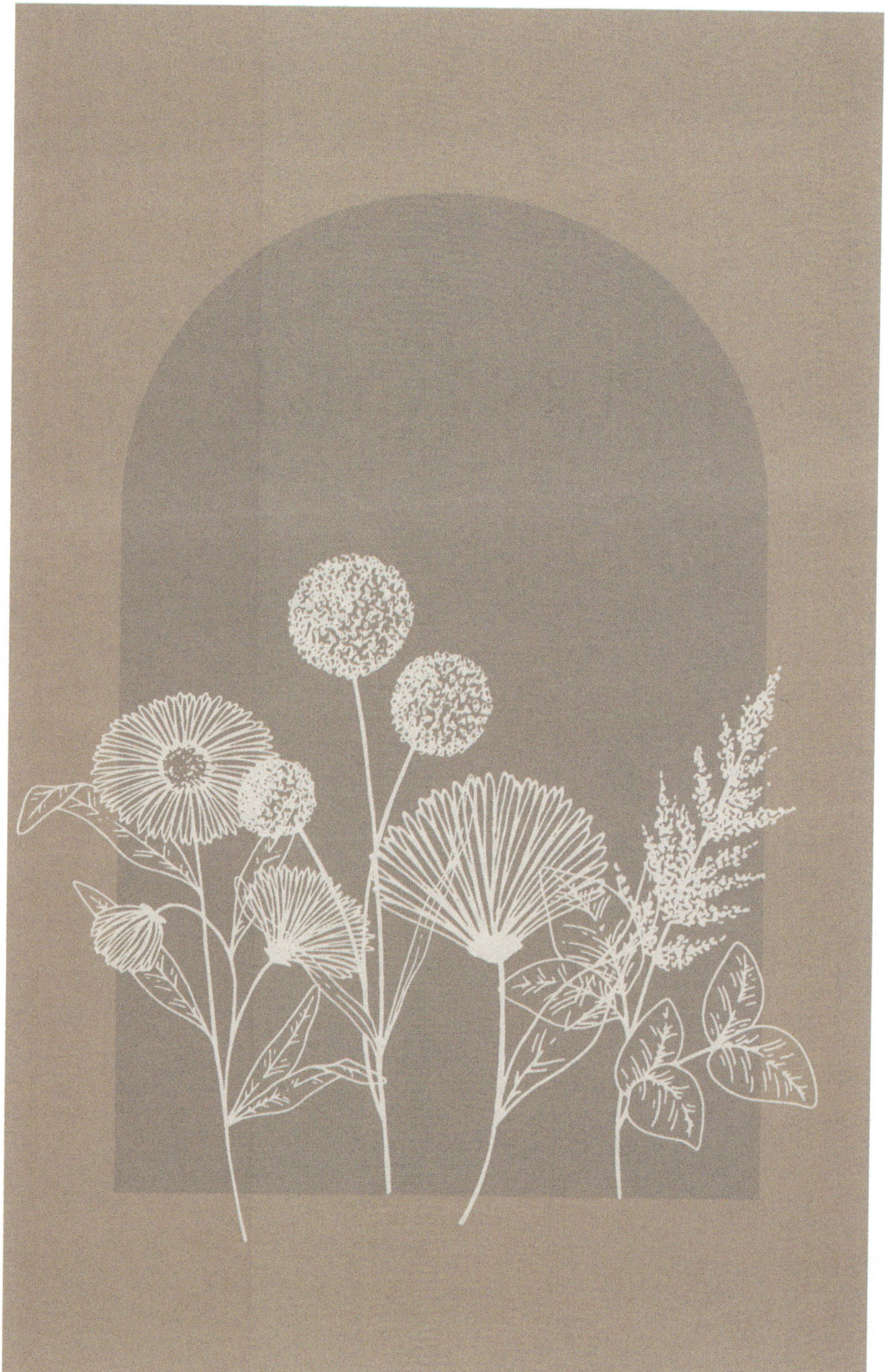

FIFTEEN

PERSPECTIVE

PATIENT FOR THE COMING PROMISE
YOUR EYES EVER ON ME
AWARE OF MY NEED
WITH AN UNDOUBTABLY GRANDER VIEW
YOU MEET ME IN THE DELAY
AFTER ALL,
IT IS FOR YOUR GLORY

"FOR THE REVELATION AWAITS AN APPOINTED TIME;
IT SPEAKS OF THE END AND WILL NOT PROVE FALSE.
THOUGH IT LINGER, WAIT FOR IT; IT WILL CERTAINLY
COME AND WILL NOT DELAY"

HABAKKUK 2:3

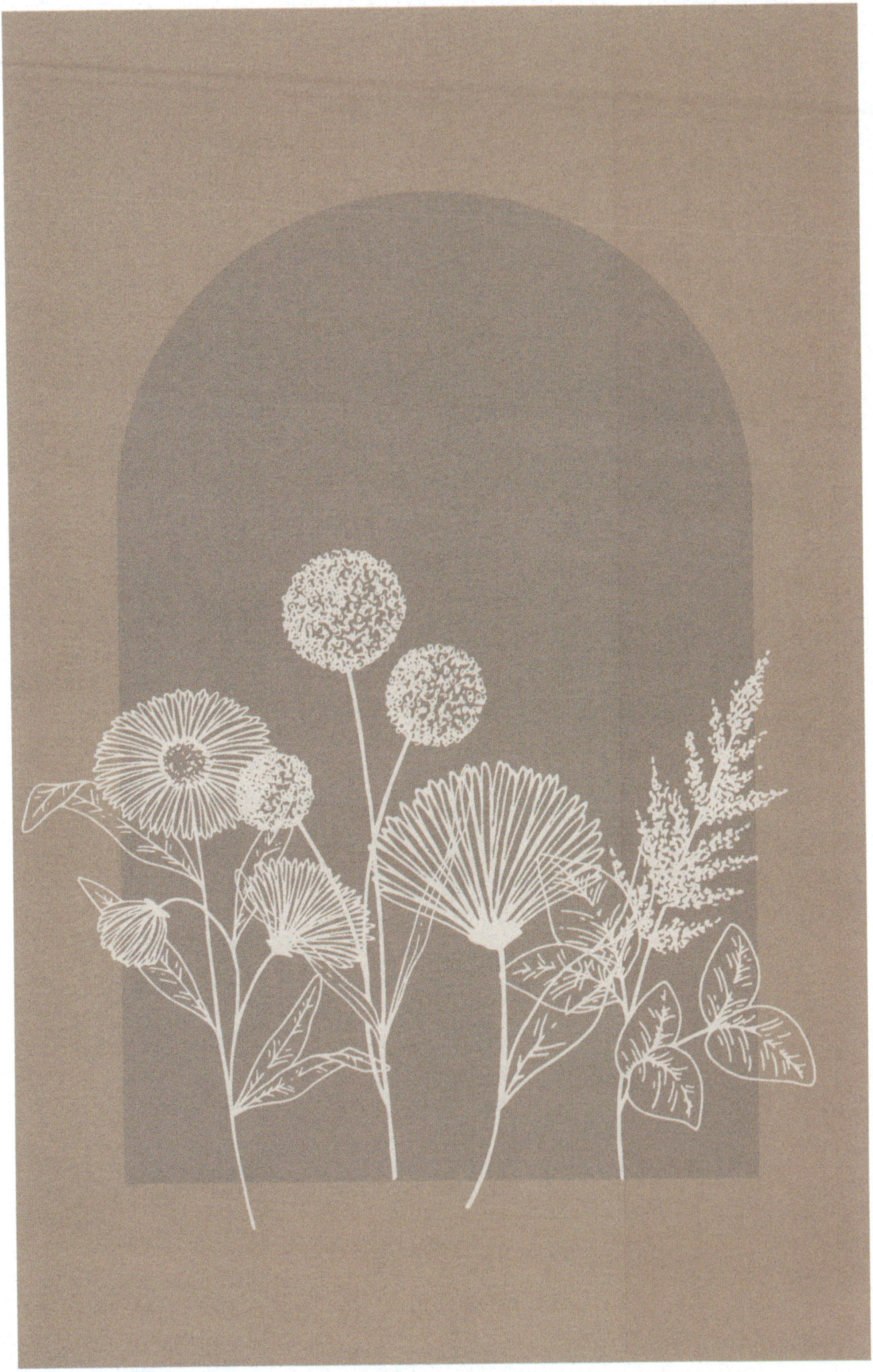

SIXTEEN

DROUGHT

OPEN HANDS
TAKE THINGS OUT
PUT THINGS IN
YOU ARE WORTHY REGARDLESS

"THOUGH THE FIG TREE DOES NOT BUD
AND THERE IS NO FRUIT ON THE VINES,
THOUGH THE OLIVE CROP FAILS
AND THE FIELDS PRODUCE NO FOOD,
THOUGH THE FLOCKS DISAPPEAR FROM THE PEN
AND THERE ARE NO HERDS IN THE STALLS,

YET I WILL CELEBRATE IN THE LORD;
I WILL REJOICE IN THE GOD OF MY SALVATION!

THE LORD MY LORD IS MY STRENGTH;
HE MAKES MY FEET LIKE THOSE OF A DEER
AND ENABLES ME TO WALK ON MOUNTAIN HEIGHTS"

HABAKKUK 3:17

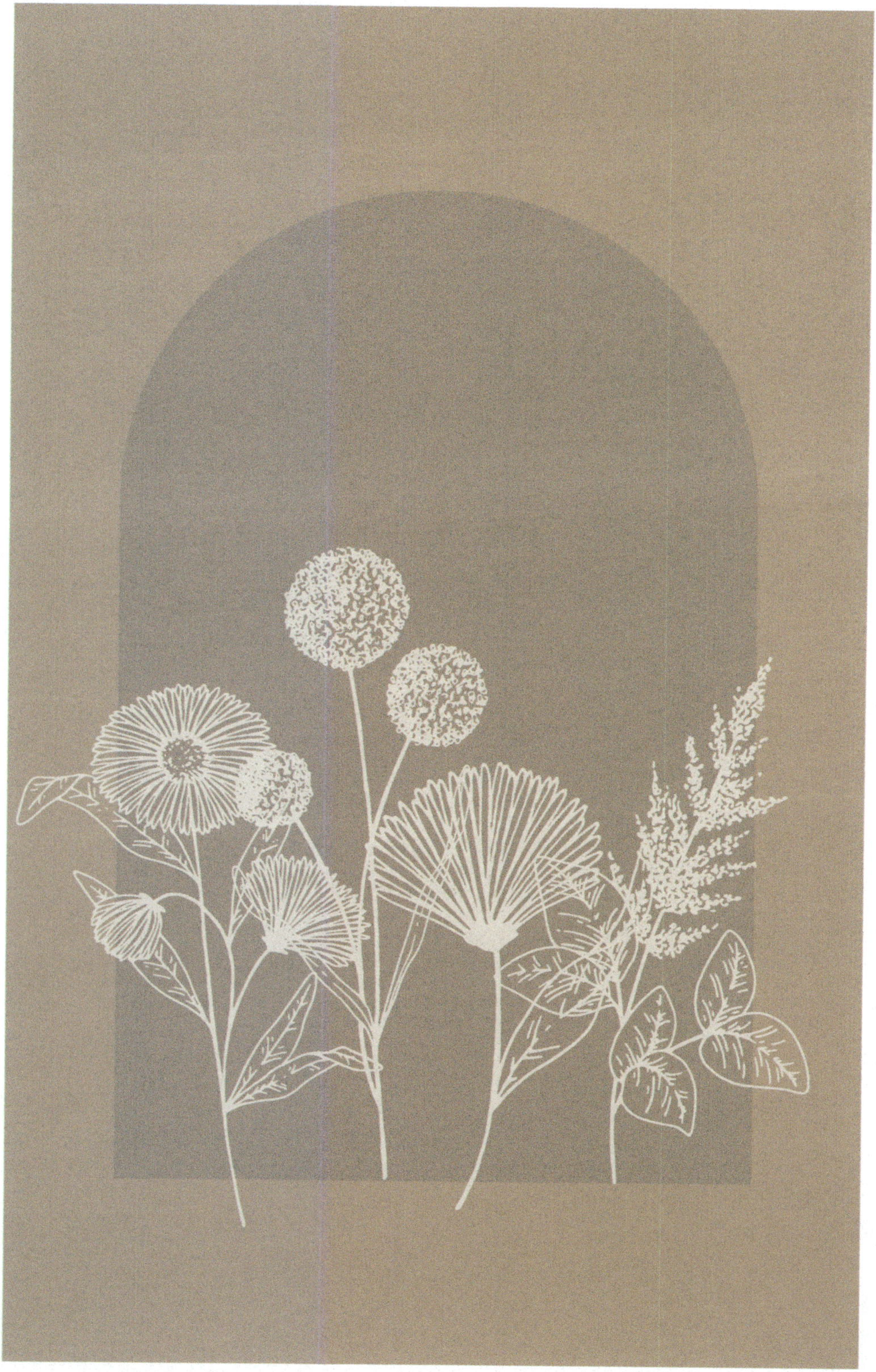

SEVENTEEN

AWAKE

YOU AWAKE MY SOUL
AND SPARK MY HEART
ONCE MORE IN THE SECRET PLACE
IS REVIVAL
STRIKE THE MATCH
ONE FLAME
LIGHTING UP THE
WHOLE HOUSE
I WILL TAKE THE
INDWELLING
WHEREVER I GO
EYES OF FIRE
I NEVER FEAR A FAINT FLICKER
FOR YOU ARE THE BURNING ONE
WHO WAKES ME UP TO LIFE ABUNDANT

I HAVE OFTEN THOUGHT TO MYSELF, "WILL THIS PASSION FADE"? "ARE MY ENTHUSIASM AND ZEAL JUST BANNERS OVER MY YOUTH"? THEN I AM REMINDED THAT HE IS THE BURNING ONE. THE ALL CONSUMING FIRE... IT IS NOT MY PORTION TO BURN OR MUSTER UP A FLAME, BUT TO LOOK INTIMATELY INTO THE EYES OF FIRE AND YIELD TO THE CONSUMING, THUS BECOMING A BURNING ONE MYSELF. THE EYES THAT ARE EVER ON MY LIFE.. THE EYES THAT NEVER LOOK ON ME WITH CONDEMNATION... BUT BURN UP THE BARRICADES THAT I HAVE BUILT WITH THIS BROKEN WORLD. ONE LOOK AT HIM.. MORNING, NOON OR NIGHT AND I CANNOT HELP BUT BECOME A TORCH....CAREFULLY HELD IN THE HANDS OF MY UNSHAKEN KING.

"THEREFORE, SINCE WE ARE RECEIVING A KINGDOM THAT CANNOT BE SHAKEN, LET US BE THANKFUL. BY IT, WE MAY SERVE GOD ACCEPTABLY, WITH REVERENCE AND AWE, FOR OUR GOD IS A CONSUMING FIRE"

HEBREWS 12:28-29

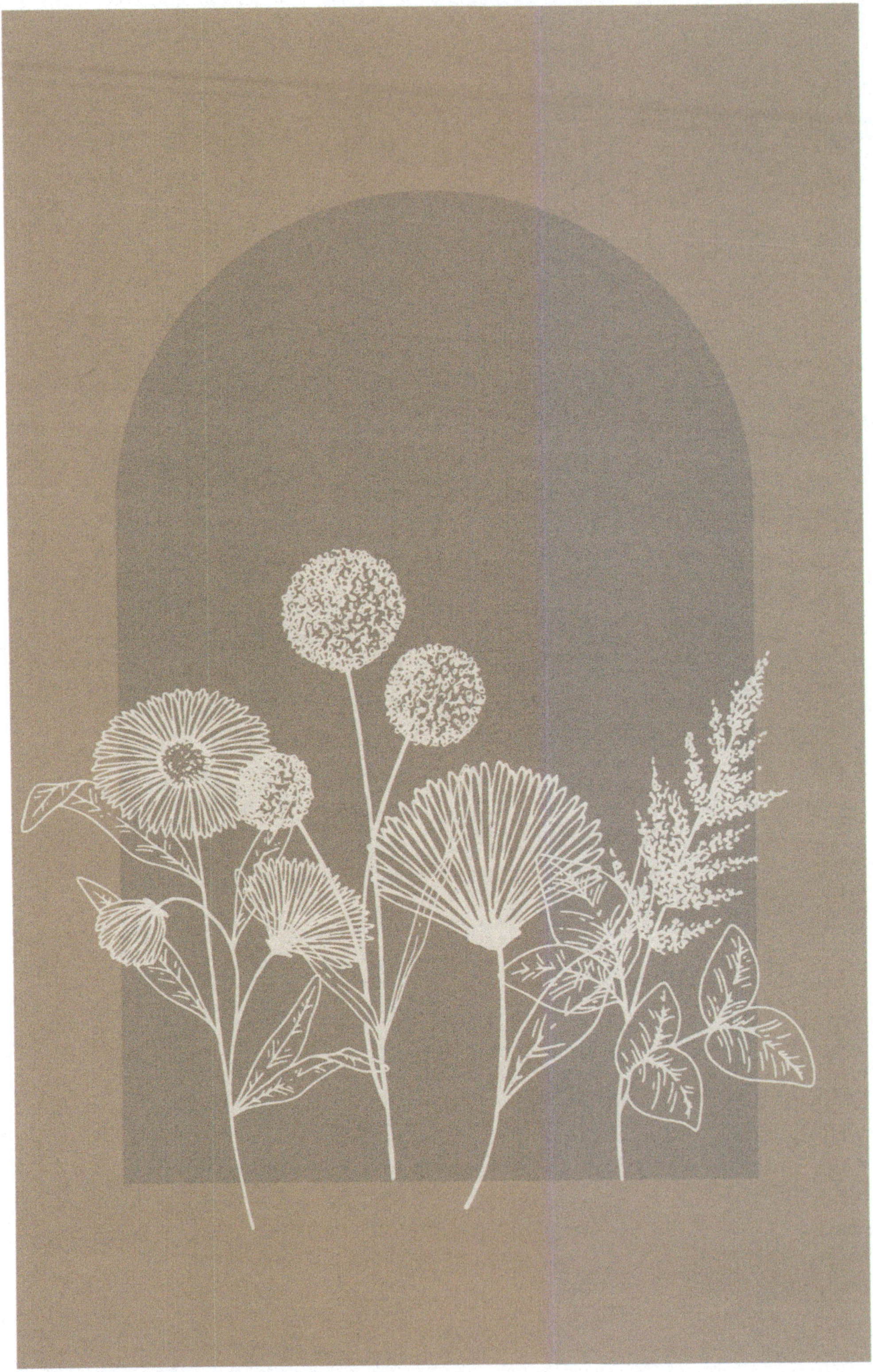

EIGHTEEN

LEAVEN

A WAY OF HEAVEN
PERMEATED, CONSUMED
THE MOST PURPOSEFUL DELAY
AN INCREASE OF THE YIELD
FROM TEARS SOWN
IN THE FIELD OF FAINT AND FERVOR
A SMALL FRACTION OF LEAVEN
TRANSFORMED
WHAT WAS NOT, TO MIRROR
ON EARTH AS IT IS IN HEAVEN

HE SAID, THEREFORE, "WHAT IS THE KINGDOM OF GOD LIKE, AND WHAT CAN I COMPARE IT TO? IT'S LIKE A MUSTARD SEED THAT A MAN TOOK AND SOWED IN HIS GARDEN. IT GREW AND BECAME A TREE, AND THE BIRDS OF THE SKY NESTED IN ITS BRANCHES."

LUKE 13:18–20

FATHER, GIVE ME A HEART THAT REJOICES IN THE SMALL BEGINNINGS, AND ONE THAT REFUSES TO DESPISE THEM

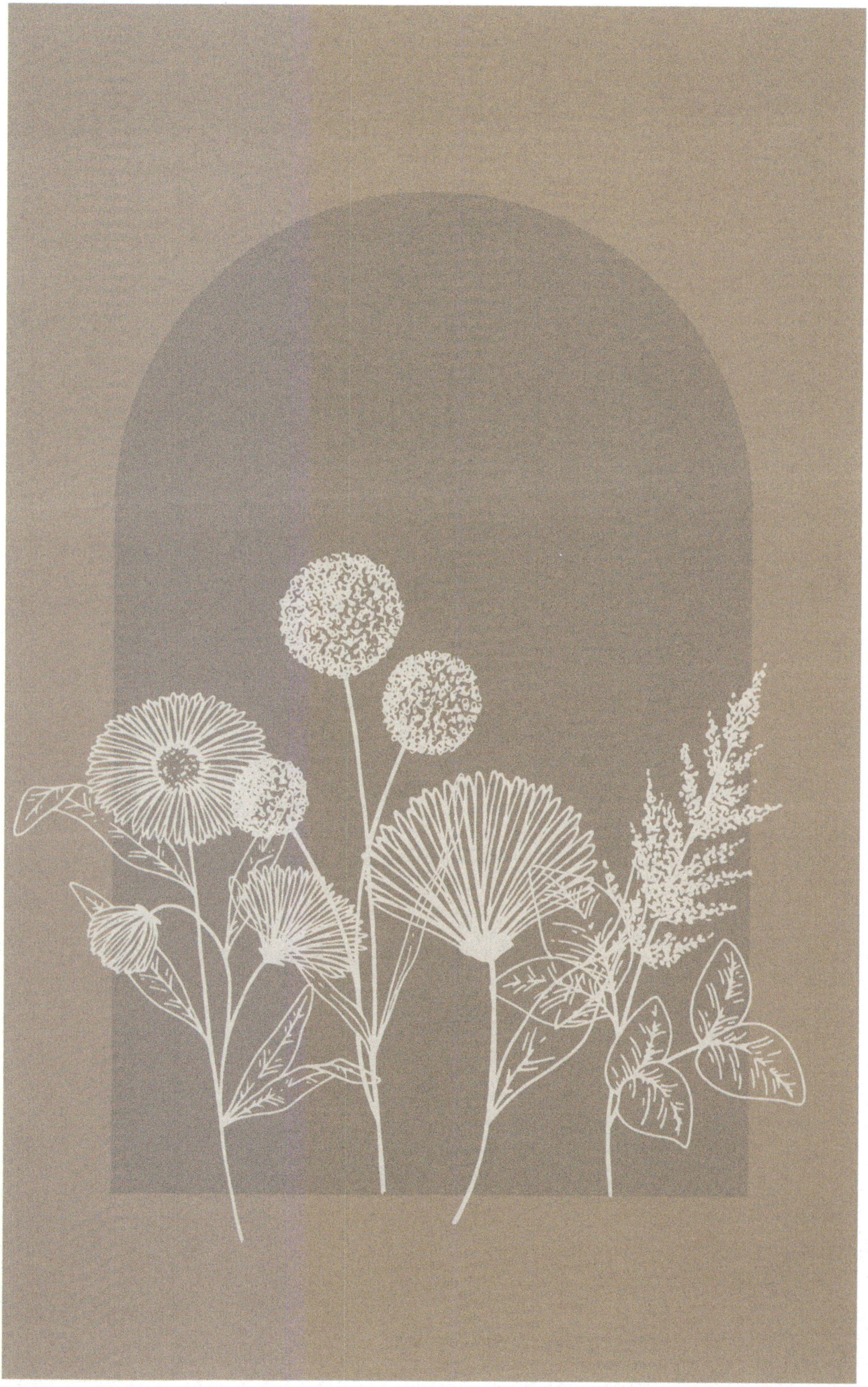

NINETEEN

FRUITFUL

YOU NEVER ACKNOWLEDGED THE
GOOD AND FRUITFUL SERVANT
WELL DONE YOU SAID
TO THE FAITHFUL ONE
THEREFORE
MY FAITHFULNESS IN THE MUNDANE
UNKNOWINGLY BEARS THE
MIRACULOUS MUCH FRUIT
FAITHFULLY INTIMATE
WITH THE UNSEEN KING
BRINGS FORTH
THE MIGHTY HARVEST
IN THE WRESTLING OF
WHAT I CANNOT SEE
ALONGSIDE MY FOREVER FRIEND
COMES THE TEEMING ORCHARD BENEATH

"HIS MASTER SAID TO HIM, 'WELL DONE, GOOD AND FAITHFUL SERVANT! YOU WERE FAITHFUL OVER A FEW THINGS; I WILL PUT YOU IN CHARGE OF MANY THINGS. SHARE YOUR MASTER'S JOY."
MATTHEW 25:23

MULTIPLY OUR MITE O GOD

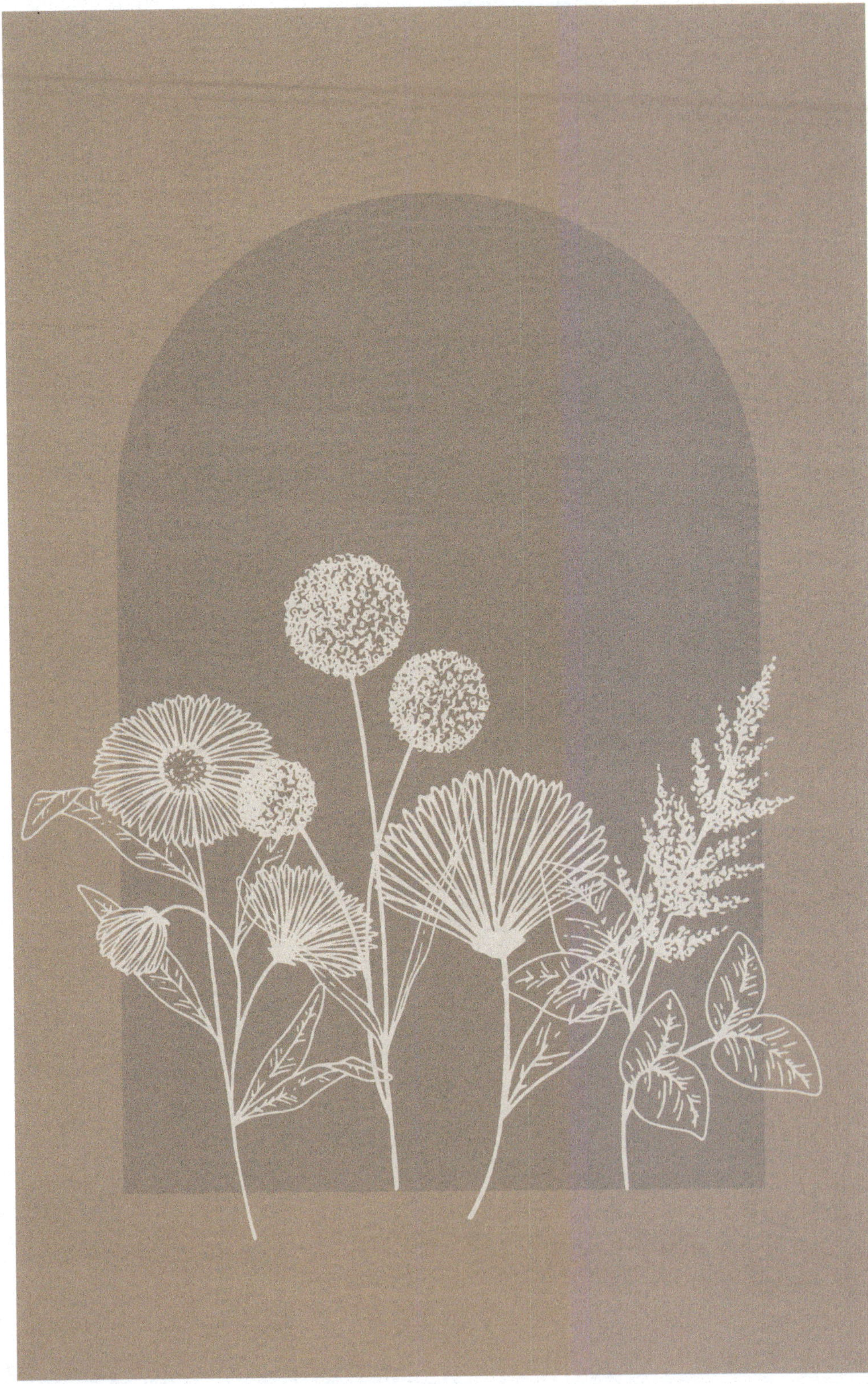

TWENTY

RISEN

WHEN I THOUGHT YOU WERE UNCONCERNED WITH MY DEFEAT
YOU SHED BLOOD AND RANSOMED THE NEW LIFE I NEEDED
READY TO FULFILL WHAT I HAD FORGOTTEN
YOU REDEEM IN THE DEAD OF NIGHT
YOU CARRY THE UNBORN DREAMS
AND THE ONES WITHERED AWAY
AS I GIVE YOU BACK
WHAT WAS GIVEN
ONCE DEAD
NOW
RISEN

"THIS IS WHAT THE LORD GOD SAYS: ON THE DAY I CLEANSE YOU FROM ALL YOUR INIQUITIES, I WILL CAUSE THE CITIES TO BE INHABITED, AND THE RUINS WILL BE REBUILT. THE DESOLATE LAND WILL BE CULTIVATED INSTEAD OF LYING DESOLATE IN THE SIGHT OF EVERYONE WHO PASSES BY. THEY WILL SAY, "THIS LAND THAT WAS DESOLATE HAS BECOME LIKE THE GARDEN OF EDEN. THE CITIES THAT WERE ONCE RUINED, DESOLATE, AND DEMOLISHED ARE NOW FORTIFIED AND INHABITED." THEN THE NATIONS THAT REMAIN AROUND YOU WILL KNOW THAT I, THE LORD, HAVE REBUILT WHAT WAS DEMOLISHED AND HAVE REPLANTED WHAT WAS DESOLATE. I, THE LORD, HAVE SPOKEN AND I WILL DO IT."

EZEKIEL 36:33-36

SIT WITH THE JEALOUS GOD WHO WANTS HIS GLORY MADE KNOWN THROUGHOUT THE WHOLE EARTH...

WHO IS MORE AWARE OF THE NEED FOR REBUILDING + REPLANTING THAN YOU EVER COULD BE

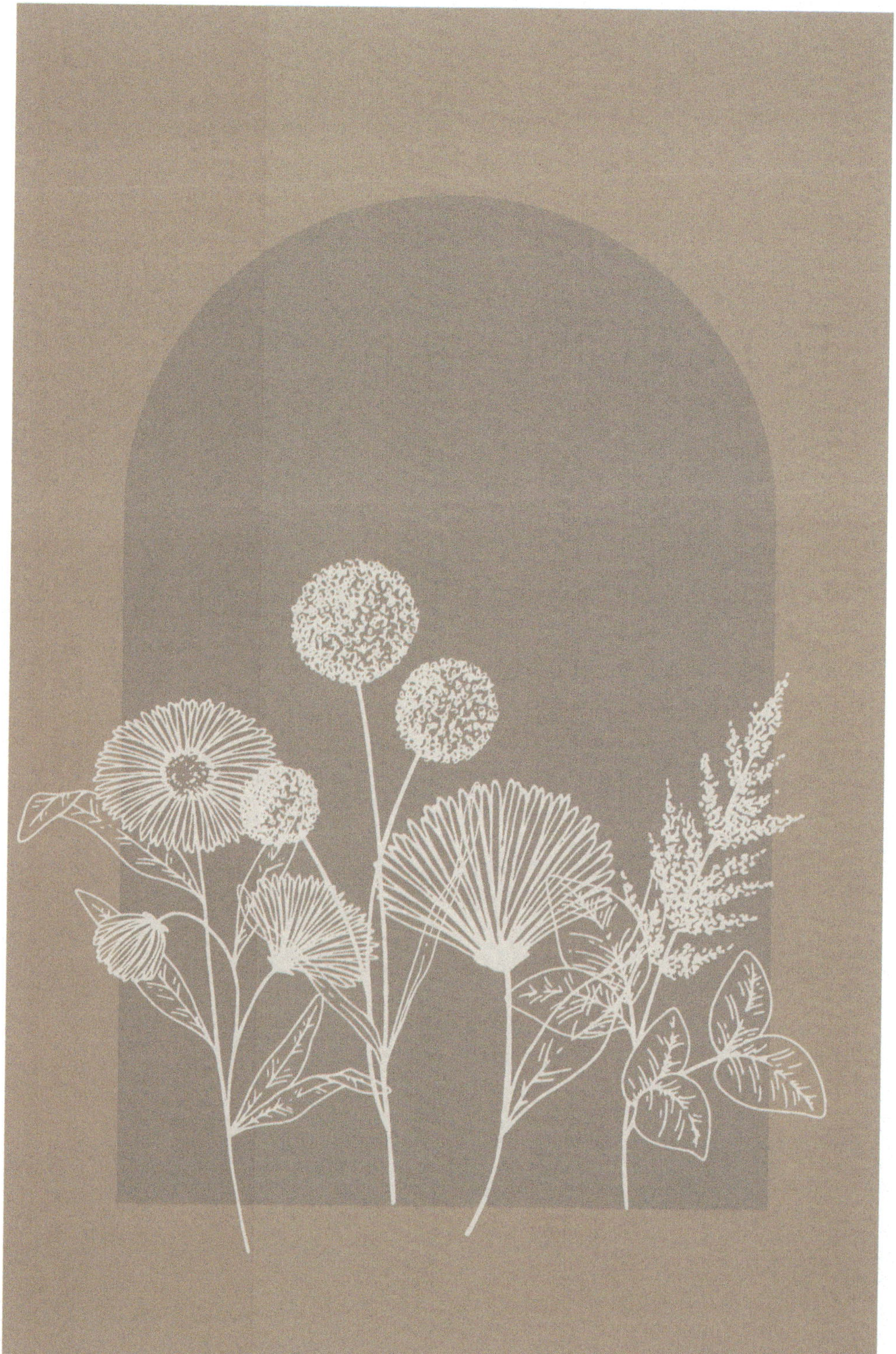

TO CLOSE,

I BLESS YOU TO BE A YIELDED ONE... TO BE ONE WHO SITS AT THE TABLE OF EXPECTANCY AND SURRENDER AND DINES WITH THE DESIRE OF THE NATIONS. HE IS THE FURTHEST THING FROM STALE AND TASTELESS. WOULD YOUR YIELDING TO HIM YIELD THE RICHEST AND SWEETEST FRUIT. FRUIT THAT LASTS...

AMEN

—SCR

YOUR KINGDOM COME,
YOU WILL BE DONE
ON EARTH
AS IT IS IN HEAVEN

CITATIONS

HOLMAN CHRISTIAN STANDARD BIBLE. B&H PUBLISHING GROUP. : BIBLICA, 2011. BIBLEGATEWAY.COM. WEB. NOV. 2021